For Theo & Lizzie
Love Grandma & Grandpa Thomas

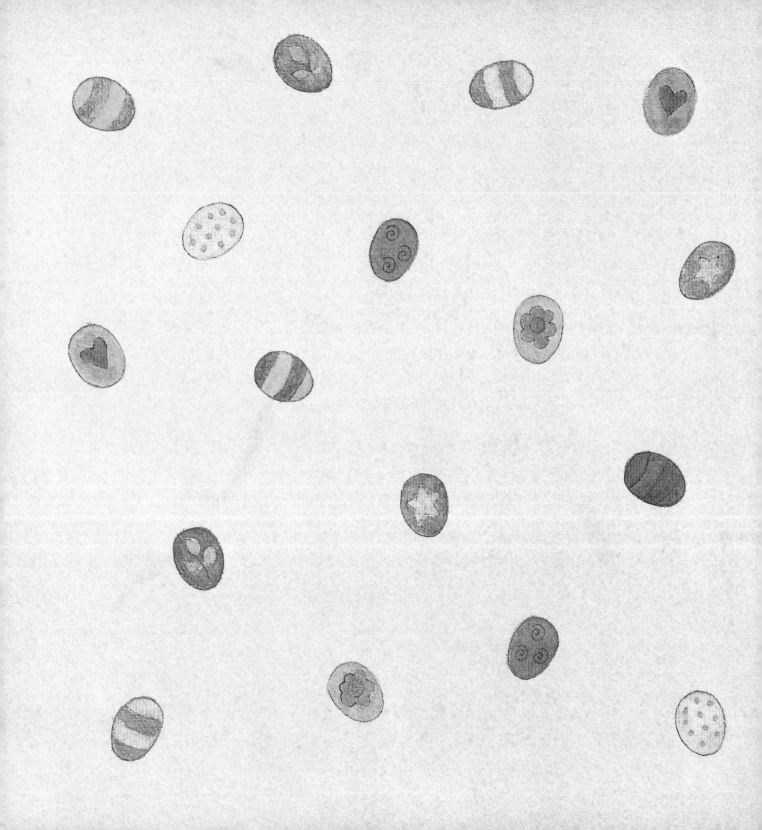

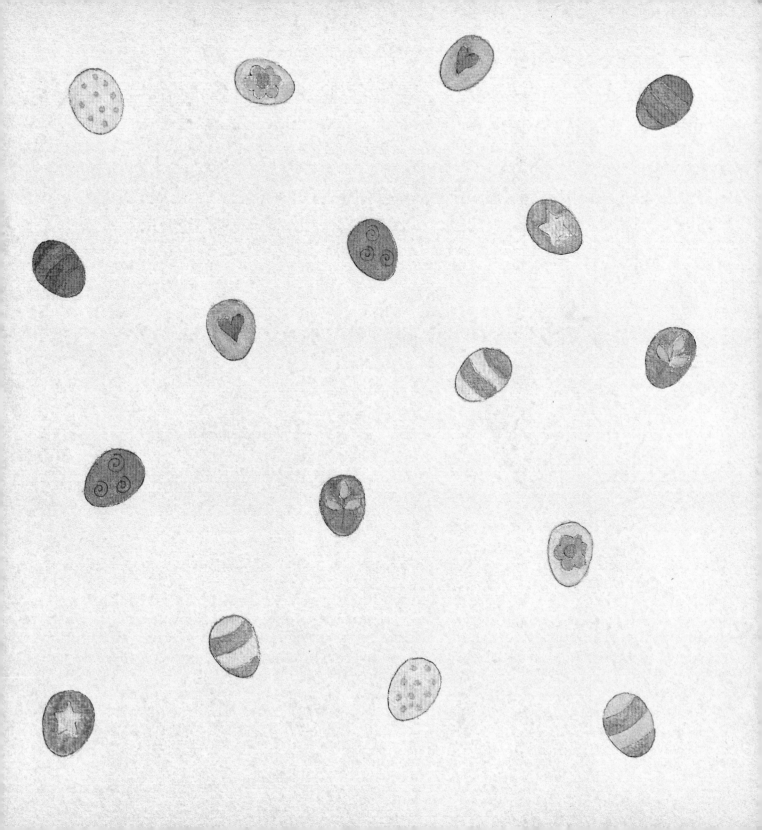

For Wendy and John – J.Z.
For Judy – J.B.C.

First edition for the United States, Canada, and the Philippines published in 2004
by Barron's Educational Series, Inc.

Hope and New Life! copyright © Frances Lincoln Limited 2004
Text copyright © Jonny Zucker 2004
Illustrations copyright © Jan Barger Cohen 2004

First published in Great Britain in 2004 by
Frances Lincoln Limited, 4 Torriano Mews,
Torriano Avenue, London NW5 2RZ
www.franceslincoln.com

All inquiries should be addressed to:
Barron's Educational Series, Inc.
250 Wireless Boulevard
Hauppauge, New York 11788
http://www.barronseduc.com

Library of Congress Catalog Card No.: 2003110644
International Standard Book No.: 0-7641-2669-5

Printed in Singapore
9 8 7 6 5 4 3 2 1

The Publishers would like to thank the Reverend Jeremy Brooks
for checking the text and illustrations.

FESTIVAL TIME!

Hope and New Life!

An Easter Story

Jonny Zucker

Illustrated by Jan Barger Cohen

It's Palm Sunday –
the beginning of Holy Week.
We remember how Jesus rode
into Jerusalem on a donkey.

On Holy Thursday, Mom, Dad, and my older sister eat bread and drink wine to remind us of Jesus' Last Supper with His disciples.

On Good Friday, we go to church
and hear how Jesus died
on the cross to save us.

We color eggs
and eat some
sticky hot cross buns.

It's Easter Sunday
and we go to church
and sing songs to celebrate
how Jesus came back to life.

I'm going on an Easter egg hunt.
The Easter bunny has hidden
colored eggs in the garden
and I find some!

Later, we watch a parade and feel happy to be celebrating our festival of hope and new life.

What Is Easter About?

Long ago, Jesus lived in Judea (now called Israel) in the region of Lake Galilee. He healed many people and taught them about God and how to live good lives.

One Sunday, He rode into Jerusalem on a donkey and all His friends walked in behind. Crowds of people came out to cheer and they cut down palm branches and waved them in celebration. We remember this happening on **Palm Sunday**, the Sunday before Easter day, and churchgoers receive a palm cross to remind them.

Four days later, on Thursday, Jesus invited His twelve friends to supper in a room upstairs in a house in Jerusalem. This is known as the **Last Supper**, because it was the last meal He ate with His friends. At supper, He broke a loaf of bread and said to His friends, "This is my body," and He took a cup of wine and said, "This is my blood." Jesus knew He was about to die and He said this so that His friends would have a way of remembering Him.

Every week in church, Christians eat bread and drink wine to remember Jesus. This is called **Holy Communion**.

After supper, Jesus went to pray in a garden with His friends. While He was there, soldiers came to arrest Him and put Him on trial before the Governor of Judea, a Roman named Pontius Pilate. Jesus' teachings frightened the Romans who were in charge, so they decided that

Jesus should die on a cross. Christians remember this on **Good Friday**. It is called Good Friday because Christians believe that when Jesus died He took away all the sins, or bad things, that we do and, as a result of His death, God forgave us. When we eat hot cross buns, we see the cross on the bun to remind us of Jesus' crucifixion.

When Jesus died, nearly all His friends were afraid and ran away, but a woman named Mary Magdalene saw where they put Jesus' body in a tomb after He died. On Sunday, she went to the tomb to look after Jesus' body. Imagine her surprise to find that the tomb was empty. She saw an angel, who told her that Jesus had come back to life again. Later, she saw Jesus for herself.

Every year, Christians remember on **Easter Sunday** that Jesus died and rose again from the dead to live forever in Heaven. Easter eggs are eaten because eggs are a sign of new life. Christians are happy at this time of year. Because Jesus came back to life, we know that we, too, can live forever with Him in Heaven.

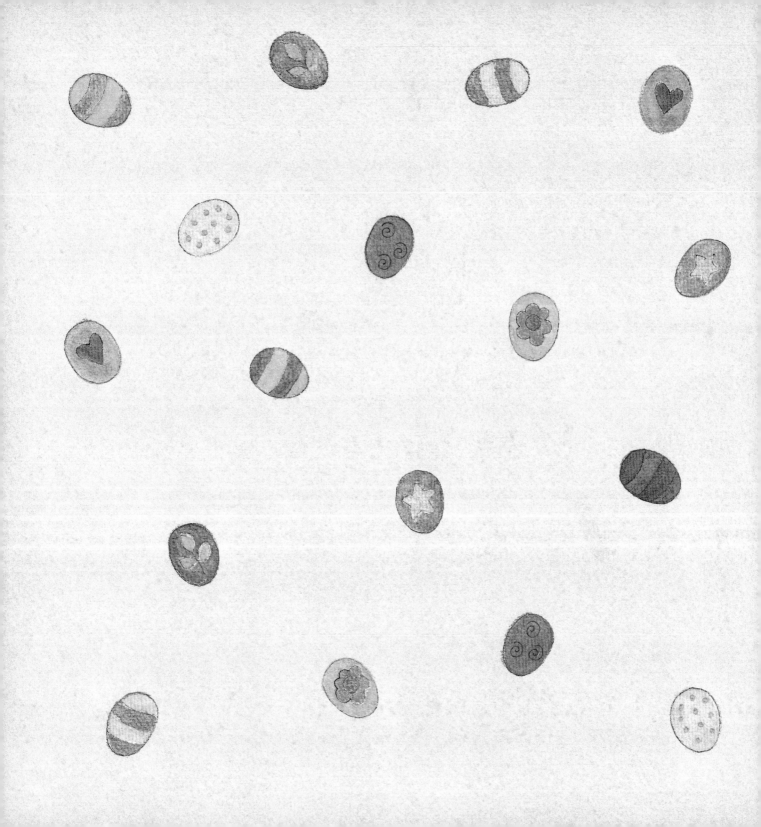

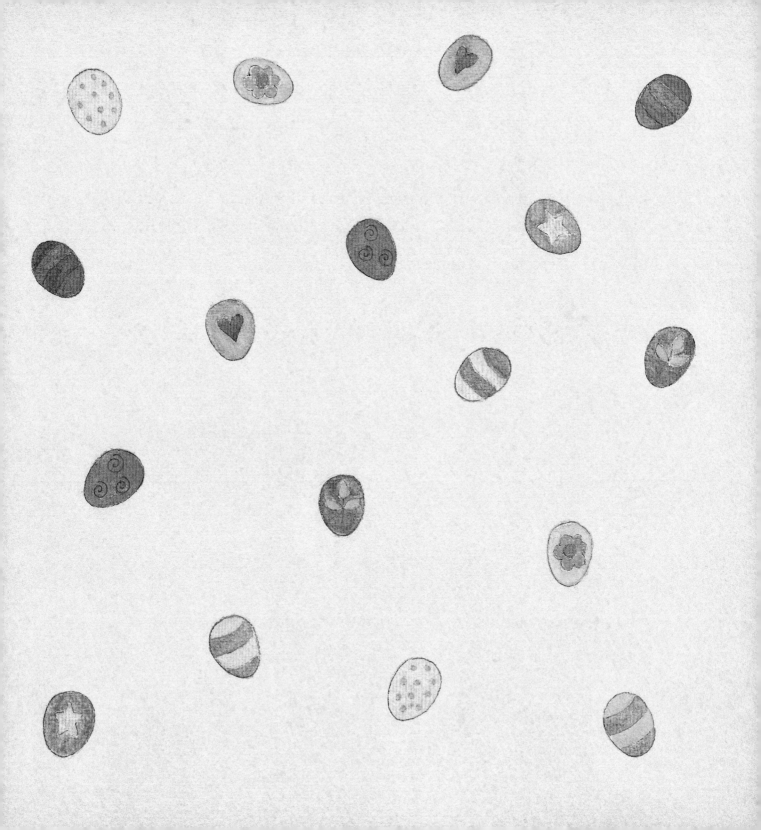